ideals® CHRISTMAS

2005

Dedicated to a celebration of the American ideals of faith in God, loyalty to country, and love of family.

Features

Departments

Cover: Artist Linda Nelson portrays the joy that children share as they celebrate the season in the painting entitled DANCING AROUND THE CHRISTMAS TREE. Copyright © Linda Nelson. All rights reserved.

Inside front cover: Artist George Hinke recalls the sleigh rides of the past and emphasizes the importance of the light of Christmas Eve. This illustration was the cover of the Christmas issue of IDEALS in 1952.

IDEALS—Vol. 62, No. 6, November 2005 IDEALS (ISSN 0019-137X, USPS 256-240) is published six times a year: January, March, May, July, September, and November by Ideals Publications, a division of Guideposts, 39 Seminary Hill Road, Carmel, NY 10512. Copyright © 2005 by Ideals Publications, a division of Guideposts. All rights reserved. The cover and entire contents of IDEALS are fully protected by copyright and must not be reproduced in any manner whatsoever. Title IDEALS registered U.S. Patent Office. Printed and bound in the USA. Printed on Weyerhauser Husky. The paper used in this publication meets the minimum requirements of American National Standard for Information Sciences—Permanence of Paper for Printed Materials, ANSI Z39.48-1984. Periodicals postage paid at Carmel, New York, and additional mailing offices. Canadian mailed under Publications Mail Agreement Number 40010140. POSTMASTER: Send address changes to IDEALS, 39 Seminary Hill Road, Carmel, NY 10512. CANADA POST: Send address changes to Guideposts PO Box 1051, Fort Erie ON L2A 6C7. For subscription or customer service questions, contact Ideals Publications, a division of Guideposts, 39 Seminary Hill Road, Carmel, NY 10512. Fax 845-228-2115. Reader Preference Service: We occasionally make our mailing lists available to other companies whose products or services might interest you. If you prefer not to be included, please write to IDEALS Customer Service.

ISBN 0-8249-1305-1 GST 893989236

Visit the *Ideals* website
at www.idealsbooks.com

The Snowstorm

Ralph Waldo Emerson

Announced by all the trumpets of the sky,
Arrives the snow, and, driving o'er the fields,
Seems nowhere to alight: the whited air
Hides hills and woods, the river, and the heaven,
And veils the farmhouse at the garden's end.
The sled and traveler stopped, the courier's feet
Delayed, all friends shut out, the housemates sit
Around the radiant fireplace, enclosed
In a tumultuous privacy of storm.
 Come see the north wind's masonry.
Out of an unseen quarry evermore
Furnished with tile, the fierce artificer
Curves his white bastions with projected roof
Round every windward stake, or tree, or door.
Speeding, the myriad-handed, his wild work
So fanciful, so savage, naught cares he
For number or proportion. Mockingly,
On coop or kennel he hangs Parian wreaths;
A swan-like form invests the hidden thorn,
Fills up the farmer's lane from wall to wall,
Maugre the farmer's sighs; and, at the gate,
A tapering turret overtops the work.
And when his hours are numbered, and the world
Is all his own, retiring, as he were not,
Leaves, when the sun appears, astonished Art
To mimic in slow structures, stone by stone,
Built in an age, the mad wind's night-work,
The frolic architecture of the snow.

Winter Trees

Nora M. Bozeman

In winter, trees wear diamonds
And powder puffs of snow;
They sunbathe in the beauty
Of snowfall's radiant glow.
Treetops don their cotton caps
After the storm takes flight;
The moon and stars shine brightly
Upon the pristine night.
Each spring trees burst out in green,
While russet trees fall brings;
But the trees that I love best
God sends on silvery wings.

An Elm's Winter Grace

Barbara True

A tree of glass and glistening grace,
A million twigs in a mirrored vice,
A pristine tower of Spanish lace,
An etching in a diamond case,
A crystal of prismatic ice
Is an elm of glistening grace.

White . . . is not a mere absence of color; it is a shining and affirmative thing, as fierce as red, as definite as black. . . . God paints in many colors; but He never paints so gorgeously, I had almost said so gaudily, as when He paints in white. —G. K. CHESTERTON

*Snow-covered trees line the shores
of Baker River in Warren, New Hampshire.
Photograph by William H. Johnson.*

*Overleaf: This myrtle tree near the Illinois River in Siskiyou National Forest, Oregon,
is beautiful even when draped with winter snow. Photograph by Steve Terrill.*

Gift of the Starlings

Wanda A. Lyday

When the warm winds of summer awaken
Each elm tree and bright maple bough,
And the white rains at noontime have shaken
Green leaves where I wander now,
Then I shall remember the starlings
That came, with no glory of song,
To cherish beneath the roofs of their wings
The earth, here where I belong.
They did what they could when the sunless
Cold lay heavy and all was bare;
Their wings fell as softly as hands that bless
Or the sound of a silver tear.
Neither green leaves, nor gold sun shall hold me,
Nor lovelier wings that have flown;
I know every leaf will descend from the tree
And the starlings again claim their own.

On Brilliant Wings

Ruth B. Field

The evergreens on the snow-hushed hill
Loomed tall and dark, cloistered and still,
Where once in the summertime's bright grace
An aria rose in the sunlit space:
The robin's cheer or the oriole,
The meadowlark from the lush, green knoll,
The cry of the linnet across the night,
The trill of the wood thrush's sheer delight.
But that was when summer graced the hill,
Where the old trees stand now sad and still.
Then suddenly, like a scrap of sky,
The jay in a bright blue arc flashed by;
And gay as the song that summer sings,
A cardinal spread its scarlet wings
To light on a tree like a lyric rhyme,
Like joy returned from the summertime.

Red Birds

Johnielu Barber Bradford

Four red birds hide
From sifting snow
Near my front door
Where cedars grow.
Four scarlet flames
Defy my gloom,
For soon I see
My cedars bloom!
No lovelier sight,
When red birds hide,
Except those specks
Close by their side—
Four dull, drab bits
Of snuggling down
Against red coats,
Four mates in brown.

Holly berries are bright against a blanket of winter snow in Multnomah County, Oregon. Photograph by Steve Terrill.

Why the Evergreen Trees Never Lose Their Leaves

A POPULAR, WHIMSICAL TALE OF KINDNESS MORE THAN A CENTURY OLD

Florence Holbrook

Winter was coming; and the birds had flown far to the south, where the air was warm and they could find berries to eat. One little bird had broken its wing and could not fly with the others. It was alone in the cold world of frost and snow. The forest looked warm, and it made its way to the trees as well as it could to ask for help.

First it came to a birch tree. "Beautiful birch tree," it said, "my wing is broken, and my friends have flown away. May I live among your branches till they come back to me?"

"No, indeed," answered the birch tree, drawing her fair green leaves away. "We of the great forest have our own birds to help. I can do nothing for you."

"The birch is not very strong," said the little bird to itself, "and it might be that she could not hold me easily. I will ask the oak." So the bird said, "Great oak tree, you are so strong, will you not let me live on your boughs till my friends come back in the springtime?"

"In the springtime!" cried the oak. "That is a long way off. How do I know what you might do in all that time? Birds are always looking for something to eat, and you might even eat up some of my acorns."

"It may be that the willow will be kind to me," thought the bird; and it said, "Gentle willow, my wing is broken, and I could not fly to the south with the other birds. May I live on your branches till the springtime?"

The willow did not look gentle then, for she drew herself up proudly and said, "Indeed, I do not know you; and we willows never talk to people whom we do not know. Very likely there are trees somewhere that will take in strange birds. Leave me at once."

The poor little bird did not know what to do. Its wing was not yet strong, but it began to fly away as well as it could. Before it had gone far, a voice was heard. "Little bird," it said, "where are you going?"

You shall live on my warmest branch all winter, if you choose.

"Indeed, I do not know," answered the bird sadly. "I am very cold."

"Come right here, then," said the friendly spruce tree, for it was her voice that had called. "You shall live on my warmest branch all winter, if you choose."

"Will you really let me?" asked the little bird eagerly.

"Indeed, I will," answered the kind-hearted spruce tree. "If your friends have flown away, it is time for the trees to help you. Here is the branch where my leaves are thickest and softest."

"My branches are not very thick," said the friendly pine tree, "but I am big and strong, and I can keep the north wind from you and the spruce."

"I can help too," said a little juniper tree. "I can give you berries all winter long, and every bird knows that juniper berries are good."

So the spruce gave the lonely little bird a home, the pine kept the cold north wind away from it, and the juniper gave it berries to eat.

The other trees looked on and talked together wisely.

"I would not have strange birds on my boughs," said the birch.

"I shall not give my acorns away for anyone," said the oak.

"I never have anything to do with strangers," said the willow; and the three trees drew their leaves closely about them.

In the morning all those shining green leaves lay on the ground, for a cold north wind had come in the night, and every leaf that it

Ice encases white pine needles in Door County, Wisconsin. Photograph by Darryl R. Beers.

touched fell from the tree.

"May I touch every leaf in the forest?" asked the wind in its frolic.

"No," said the frost king. "The trees that have been kind to the little bird with the broken wing may keep their leaves."

This is why the leaves of the spruce, the pine, and the juniper are always green.

The Christmas Rose

Loise Pinkerton Fritz

When all the fields are winter lined
And brooks are frozen over,
When snowflakes trim the lofty pines
And days move forward slower,
When all the earth's December strewn,
The Christmas rose is then in bloom.

Winter Patterns

Mildred L. Jarrell

It's early morn and round about
Jack Frost has been so early out
Painting all the windows bright,
Tinting with his brush of white.
A gnarled old tree is bending down,
Rigid in her icy gown.
Meadowland's a frosty glow;
Earth lies sleeping 'neath the snow;
Crystal laces trim the hedge;
Scallops rim the window ledge;
Fairy patterns grace the door;
Wintertime is here once more.

Christmas waves a
magic wand over this world,
and, behold, everything is
softer and more beautiful.
—Norman Vincent Peale

*The morning sun gently touches aspens near a house
in the Sierra Nevada Mountains in California.
Photograph by Londie Padelsky.*

BACKYARD CALENDAR

Joan Donaldson

Nestling my hands in my mittens, I gaze over the garden gate. Last night's snowfall caps the cedar posts and ices the wooden slats, forming a lace edging that circles the garden. Mounds of snow cushion the rose arbor. Although the air is now still, during the storm the wind blew inches of snow into rippling dunes and tiny whirlpools carved depressions around the pipe of the water spigot.

On this shortest day of the year, cold sharpens the air and the sun seems to stand still in the gentian-blue sky. The single digits marked on the thermometer and the calf-deep snow defy the fact that, after today, the earth moves

---

Cherry red rosehips hang like ornaments on the large shrub roses.

---

toward spring. For these brief months, the land rests beneath a glistening comforter; and I must wait for the days to grow longer and warmer before I can slip my fingers in the soil again.

I am not the first to visit this sheltered spot. Sometime after the clouds passed, a rabbit squeezed through a gap that I have yet to discover. Its feet dimpled the surface as it zigzagged across the buried garden beds, sniffing for a scrap of cabbage or carrot. Come spring, I will need to find that gap before I plant my rows of peas.

Goldfinches chatter from the drooping sunflowers, and they toss bits of seeds and shells that speckle the snow already etched by bird tracks. Near the gate, I see an imprint of wings where a junco swayed on the bent cane of a rose bush before ascending to the refuge of a nearby pine.

Bare of leaves and bristling with thorns, the branches of the roses nestle against the fence, offering the only color on this midwinter day. Cherry red rosehips hang like ornaments on the large shrub roses. Tiny ruby beads shine at the ends of the Scotch rose's branches. The maroon and gray rose branches overlap as they wreath the garden, forming a garland decorated with red rosehips. In March, the early robins will feast on these fruits that linger above the drifts.

Finally, I lift my snow shovel and begin to scoop, freeing the garden gate from the flood of snow. I toss the fluff aside and dig a ribbon of a path to my cold frames. Snow drapes the sloping wooden rectangles that run along one bed. Carefully, I clean off the plexiglass sashes and wipe them with my mittens. Eight inches below the frosted window, red-speckled lettuce and rosettes of soft-green mache glow against the brown soil. A few brave heads of romaine reach toward the light. I stifle my yearnings to lift the windows in order to pull a few weeds and inhale the fragrance of damp earth, a gardener's perfume. With such cold temperatures, I can merely view the progress of my plantings. But

Rosehips ornament the winter snow in a garden in Green Bay, Wisconsin. Photograph by Darryl R. Beers.

on New Year's Day, I will reward my present self-control and pick from among these offerings to make a salad to celebrate fresh beginnings of the emerging year.

*The earth holds her breath.
The land slumbers.*

Soon, January blizzards will deposit high ridges of snow; and these seedlings will wait snugly beneath the layers of snowy insulation. Sitting at my kitchen table, I will listen to the wind shake the trees and, with a stack of seed catalogs, satisfy my longings to dig in the dirt.

In midwinter, when dark and light wrestle, waiting for spring sometimes is the hardest work for a gardener. But I have learned that after snowstorms sweep over my garden a pristine beauty follows. The earth holds her breath. The land slumbers. I rejoice knowing that, one day, the gray skies will flee as the snowy months melt into spring. The earth's pulse will quicken and my garden will bloom once more.

Joan Donaldson is the author of a picture book and a young adult novel, as well as essays that have appeared in many national publications. She and her husband raised their sons on Pleasant Hill Farm in Michigan, where they continue to practice rural skills.

A Country Youth Talks about a City Man

Patience Eden

He's never felt the handle of an ax
Grooving his shoulder as he's climbed the hill
Of pasture to the woods; nor left his tracks
In crusty morning snow; nor breathed the still,
Cold air of six o'clock; nor watched the sun
Tingeing the eastern clouds to rose and amber.
Think—he's never had the fun
Of shaking pine boughs till the whole air snows
About him and the silly rabbits gaze,
Their ears erect as paddles, while they sit
Behind a log, all in a slant-eyed daze
Of witless indecision!
Think—he's never watched the drag tooth on a saw
Pull out the roll of sawdust from a spruce,
(The crosscut one, I mean) or smelled the raw,
Sweet flesh of standing wood,
        the pungent juice of gum,
Or heard the ice, so tissue-thin,
That stars ray out in needles, splintered white,
When blobs of snow fall down and make a din
Of crystal jangling, delicate and bright.
He's never walked the homeward, tired mile,
Taking his morning's tracks the shortest way
And at his supper boasted with a smile,
"I bet I've cut a cord of wood today!"

Barns are scattered throughout Indian Valley
in the Northern Sierra Nevada Mountains in California.
Photograph by Carr Clifton.

SNOW PAINTING
Mary C. Ferris

The canvas is ready, the slope gleaming white,
Freshly covered with snowfall the previous night.
And now for the colors, the greens and the reds,
The bright little snowsuits of children with sleds.
In cap and mitt brilliant as wool can be dyed,
They weave in and out and they tumble and slide
Framed by my window, a picture that cheers
The grave and sedate hearts of our grown-up years.

THE PRESENCE OF SNOW
Eileen Spinelli

In the presence of snow,
weeds
become flowers,
fields
become
laughing feather beds.
In the presence of snow,
overcoats
fall to wings,
strangers
become angels.
Peace
becomes a familiar song,
in the presence of snow.

SLEIGHING SONG
John Shaw

When calm is the night and the stars shine bright,
The sleigh glides smooth and cheerily;
And mirth and jest abound,
While all is still around,
Save the horses' trampling sound
And the horse-bells tinkling merrily.

Snowshoes and a warm green sweater make a winter still life.
Photograph by Nancy Matthews.

SLICE OF LIFE

Edgar A. Guest

SLEIGH BELLS

In forty years we've changed the world
And traded many things.
We've banished glowing stoves to gain
The warmth a furnace brings.
We've polished off discomforts with
Invention's magic art;
We've built the "press-the-button" age
When countless motors start.
But thinking of my boyhood days,
We lost a joy, I'll say,
When faithful horse and cutter were
Forever put away.
For when there comes a fall of snow,
I find for them I mourn
And that strap of tinkling sleigh bells
Supplanted with a horn.

We give up youth for mellow age;
Each forward step we take
To reach a joy which lies ahead
An old charm we forsake.
We deal and barter through the years
Old customs for the new,
Find easier ways to do the tasks
Once difficult to do.
But sometimes as we move along
To build the better day,
We learn we've been compelled to throw
A lovely thing away.
And thinking of my boyhood days
To this I will be sworn:
Sleigh bells sang a prettier song
Than any motor horn.

A little girl is encouraged by an older brother to enjoy her first adventure on a sled in this painting by Robert Duncan entitled EMMA'S SLEIGH RIDE. Copyright © Robert Duncan. Image provided by Robert Duncan Studios. All rights reserved.

I do come home at Christmas. We all do, or we all should. We all come home, or ought to come home, for a short holiday—the longer, the better—from the great boarding school where we are forever working at our arithmetical slates, to take, and give a rest. —Charles Dickens

Hitch Old Dobbin to the Sleigh
Mamie Ozburn Odum

Hitch Old Dobbin to the sleigh;
We're going home today,
To holidays of long ago
Once more to romp and play.

There'll be fires of blazing logs,
Candlelight, and drifting snow,
With Grandpa and our Grandma
To grace the old wood door.

Oh, what a joyous greeting,
Halls trimmed in gold and green,
Tall trees with lights and glitter
Of every hue and sheen.

We're going home for Christmas
Where the cakes are spicy sweet,
With nuts and pies and candies
And a turkey stuffed to eat.

Hitch Old Dobbin to the sleigh;
Feel frosty winds of morn.
Listen! Hear the church bells ring,
Proclaiming Christ was born.

Christmastime, we're going home,
Sleighbells ringing all the way;
We'll sing songs as we glide along
This merry Christmas Day.

*The Cilleyville Covered Bridge is part of the **charm of** Potter Place, New Hampshire. Photograph by William H. Johnson.*

Inset: A Christmas wreath glows with warm lights and a gold bow. Photograph by William H. Johnson.

SOMEONE TO REMEMBER

Richard Keller

MY GRANDFATHER'S WORKSHOP

Those shoes," a fan once said, "I love those shoes." After many years of working as an illustrator, I am often asked where I find my design ideas. The particular shoes this person liked are those sandals that the Thingumajig family wears in the books that my wife Irene wrote and that I illustrated. The Thingumajigs' oversized sandals are actually a humorous tribute to the skills of my paternal grandfather, a professional shoe-maker. Today, after many years of perfecting my own skills as an illustrator and sculptor, I have come to realize that my interest in art began with my grandfather's shoe shop and my Aunt Magdalene's love of family and holidays.

It was shortly after Christmas of 1928 that my mother died of pneumonia, and my father and I moved to Chicago to live with my grandparents and my maiden aunt, Magdalene.

My grandfather was a tall man with a small moustache and white hair, and he loved his craft of shoemaking very much. His shop was behind the garden at the back of the house. In those days, many professional people had their shoes custom-made because they were on their feet much of the time during a working day. People like doctors, store managers, police officers, mail carriers, and others needed sturdy, comfortable shoes. My grandfather's shoe shop was magical. I can still see him working: cutting leather, gluing and nailing heels, sewing soles to old worn shoes and boots,

and polishing and buffing them to look like new. Even the smell of rubber cement became pleasant to me. I found that workshop a very comforting and peaceful place to be, and I spent many hours watching Grandfather create something from nothing—a form of art.

One day my grandfather was away from the shop. What an invitation for a little boy who wanted to emulate his idol! I went into the shop and made a miniature, elf-like shoe, complete with heel and laces; it was only about three inches long. Even for a boy of five, I had strong arms, and I was able to manipulate my grandfather's knife and scis-

---

I went into the shop and made a miniature, elf-like shoe.

---

sors and complete my project. When he returned to find that I had touched his tools and materials, he was definitely not pleased; I was forbidden to make any more uninvited visits to the shop.

Inside Grandfather's shop were two domed miniatures that also fascinated me. They had been purchased at the 1893 World Columbian Exposition in Chicago and occupied a special place on the counter. One was a mass of wheels, gears, and levers attended by tiny shoemakers, an artist's idea of a shoe manufacturing plant. The second glass miniature was a building construc-tion site that had small figures sawing and hammering and lifting timbers. Both structures were about twenty inches tall by ten inches round. These two pieces were truly works of art that I never tired of studying.

That first Christmas at my grandparents' home was, of course, memorable. Aunt Magdalene loved all the holidays, but Christmas was her favorite. While I was asleep in my bed, the piano bench was moved near the dining room table for extra seating and the Christmas tree was put up in the living room. My grandparents and my aunt had been up most of the night wrapping presents. The sight of the tree on Christmas morning filled me with awe. Today I still remember the profusion of twinkling lights, ornaments, and garlands as well as the sweet smell of freshly cut pine that mingled with aromas emanating from the kitchen. My grandmother had just brewed coffee, fried bacon, made French toast, and squeezed orange juice. Later that day, all the aunts and uncles and cousins joined us. The entire day was filled with laughter and good cheer, reminiscent of Dickens' *A Christmas Carol*. I really felt a deep sense of belonging and much warmth among my family, with my grandfather at the head of all these nice people.

When my grandfather died, I was only ten years old; but even then I understood that he would always be important to my life. I painted a portrait of him and made a frame of scrap wood to

The Thingumajigs make a comical chorus in this illustration from SANTA VISITS THE THINGUMAJIGS. *Copyright © by Richard Keller.*

which I glued tools and items from his workshop, such as pieces of wooden pegs he used for heels, nails, leather, and sewing needles. My grandfather's room became my bedroom, and I hung the portrait I had made where I could see it every day.

Years later, as an adult, I discovered that those memories of my grandfather's home and his shop became important to me in a different way. After I married my British-born wife, Irene, who was an editor and a prolific writer, she and I visited York. An excavation was in progress along the riverside in the middle of the town, and artifacts of an earlier civilization were discovered. One intriguing item was a very simple leather sandal with long, trailing thongs cut from one piece. Irene and I began to visualize a character that just might wear such a shoe, something like an elf or a troll. But he would definitely be a creature full of mischief, and so a "Thingumajig" was born!

Irene created the stories and wrote the verses about the silly antics and situations of the Thingumajig creatures. She had always said that she wanted "to give the world a giggle." I conceived the illustrations, and, on each page, the distinctive attire of these creatures is their long, detailed footwear, sometimes sandals and sometimes fancy shoes with buckles and boots. My grandfather would laugh at the footwear, certainly, but he would also be proud that his grandson remembers the craft of making leather shoes.

Christmas Greeting
Author Unknown

Sing hey! Sing hey!
For Christmas Day;
Twine mistletoe and holly,
For friendship glows
In winter snows,
And so let's all be jolly.

A Catch
by the Hearth
Author Unknown

Sing we all merrily;
Christmas is here,
The day that we love best
Of days in the year.

Bring forth the holly,
The box, and the bay;
Deck out our cottage
For glad Christmas Day.

Sing we all merrily;
Draw around the fire,
Sister and brother,
Grandsire and sire.

This doorstep welcomes visitors with pyracantha and holly decorations. Photograph by Larry LeFever/Grant Heilman.

27

> Cherish your human
> connections:
> your relationships with
> friends and family.
> —BARBARA BUSH

Homeward

Alice Kennelly Roberts

Our day's long search had ended
As evening shadows fell
And brought a triumph to the heart
Which words could never tell;
For though the cold nipped sharply
At fingers, ears, and toes,
We had our tree for Christmas
And now sought night's repose.

The last mile was the longest,
So very tired were we.
Dad pulled the sled; I held the tree,
And, then, home we could see.
Across the snow-swept distance
Our sleepy village lay,
With warmth of friends and loved ones
And happy Christmas Day.

How like our life's long journey,
The trail which Time has made.
The loved ones waiting for us,
The scenes which never fade,
The strength of Someone near us
To lift the heavy load—
These are memories we keep
To cherish on life's road.

*Lovely Christmas quilts and a friendly snowman
welcome family and friends in Diane Phelan's
painting entitled* COUNTRY CHRISTMAS. *Copyright*

HOMETOWN AMERICA

Patricia A. Pingry

LAMAR, MISSOURI

When I come "home," I fly into Kansas City, then drive 120 miles straight south on US 71 to the flat plains of southwestern Missouri and the town of Lamar. Along the highway lie the wheat fields over which the ubiquitous hawks "make lazy circles in the sky." To the west, a network of strip mines filled with water and fish has become a summertime hangout for swimmers and anglers. But I turn east at the US 71 and 160 junction and head for home.

I pass the field that once held prize-winning mules. Mules are important to my state, having pulled plows and wagons and thus became the force by which Missouri was settled and farmed; we take seriously the adage "stubborn as a mule." The mules that once roamed this farm were honored by an invitation to the inaugural parade of 1949—that of Missouri native Harry S. Truman.

Truman's birthplace is the most publicized site in this town of four thousand people or so. The Truman family lived here only a short time before moving to Independence, where Truman remained until his death. But the tiny, white frame house is where Truman began life and is open to the public.

In ten minutes, I am on the square. Lamar is the county seat of Barton County and the late nineteenth-century courthouse is one of the loveliest. The land on which it sits extends far beyond the building; and the grassy lawn and large trees give this edifice a sense of grandeur.

When I was growing up, the square was not only the geographical center of town, but also the community hub. I took my driver's test at the courthouse, then flunked my first driving exam. With a highway patrolman wearing his "Smokey-the-Bear" hat seated next to me, this sixteen-year-old just could not parallel park well enough to pass the first time. Throughout school summer vacations, every Saturday evening found me with the high school band at the covered bandstand on the courthouse lawn, where we played an hour's concert for the shoppers.

For one week every September, the square

I walked along the snow-covered sidewalks and window-shopped along the square.

---

became the midway for the county fair. The old memorial hall held the pies, cakes, quilts, tomatoes, and other typical fair entries for judging. Two of the blocks just off the square became the tented and temporary barns for the cattle, horses, and pigs that were judged on Saturday morning.

That afternoon, a parade, led by the high school band and replete with floats from organizations and businesses, brought the week's flurry of activity to a culmination. But by then, the whole town smelled like a barnyard. The route to church on Sunday morning lay amid the remains of cotton candy cones and leftover horse straw.

The Barton County Courthouse is decorated for the holidays. Photograph courtesy of Patricia Pingry.

At Christmastime, the light poles around the square held colored lights and tinsel; a manger scene stood on the courthouse lawn. On many dark evenings after church choir practice or my piano lesson, I walked along the snow-covered sidewalks and window-shopped along the square. Then, even the closest cities seemed so far away that we shopped on the square whose lighted store windows displayed clothes or gifts. The sounds of Christmas music played the whole month of December; and Bing Crosby's "White Christmas" and Mario Lanza's "We Three Kings" followed me the three blocks home.

Today, Lamar's courthouse still stands, cleaned of the grime of a hundred years; the lawn remains groomed and its trees bloom every spring. The county fair still kicks off each autumn. The park, south of the square, has the same shelters where my vacation Bible school held its annual picnic; and the park's little stream where we caught tadpoles and crawdads still winds through its grounds. The school, north of the square, still stands on the land to which I walked every morning and from which I walked every afternoon. Tom Wolfe said we can't go home again; but I prefer the sentiments of Walt Whitman:

> There was a child went forth every day;
> And the first object he looked upon, that object
>   he became;
> And that object became part of him. . . .
> These became part of that child who went forth
>   every day, and who now goes, and will always
>   go forth every day.

After all these years and living in many towns in the U.S. and Europe, I still retain some "Lamar." I have the same plainspokenness that typifies the lower Midwesterner and the stubborn "show-me" attitude of the native Missourian. But Lamar gave me something more important: a sense of community, that early certainty of belonging that only a small town can provide. This is that which "became part of [this] child who went forth every day, and who now goes, and will always go forth every day."

FAMILY RECIPES

HUNGARIAN FILLED COOKIES

Phyllis M. Peters, Three Rivers, Michigan

1 cup butter, softened
2 3-ounce packages cream
   cheese, softened
2 cups flour
   Strawberry preserves
   Confectioners' sugar

Preheat oven to 350°F. In a large bowl, cream butter and cheese. Add flour and mix well. On a floured board, roll out dough into a 10- x 6-inch rectangle. Cut into 15 two-by-two-inch squares. Place ¼ teaspoon preserves in center of each square. Pull the opposite corners together and pinch to secure. Bake 15 minutes or until golden. Remove from oven and cool. Sprinkle with confectioners' sugar. Makes 15 cookies.

KRINGLA

Margaret Anderson, Dunkerton, Iowa

4 cups flour
1½ teaspoons baking soda
2 teaspoons baking powder
½ teaspoon salt
1 cup sugar
½ cup shortening
1 egg
1 cup buttermilk
½ cup sweetened, condensed milk
   Colored sugar

Preheat oven to 400°F. In a medium bowl, sift together flour, baking soda, baking powder, and salt. Set aside. In a large bowl, cream sugar with shortening. Add egg, buttermilk, and condensed milk; beat well. Gradually add flour mixture to butter mixture, mixing well. Shape dough into a ball and cover with plastic wrap; refrigerate overnight. On a lightly floured board, thinly roll one tablespoon dough into a 6- x ¼-inch length. Shape into a figure eight and place on an ungreased cookie sheet. Repeat for remaining dough. Bake 10 minutes or until golden. Sprinkle with colored sugar; cool. Store in a tightly covered container. Makes 48 cookies.

With these recipes from IDEALS' readers, you can enjoy the cherished tradition of sharing cookies with friends and family. We would love to try your favorite recipe too. Send a typed copy to Ideals Publications, 535 Metroplex Drive, Suite 250, Nashville, Tennessee 37211. Payment will be provided for each recipe published.

MOTHER'S TEA CAKES
Willena Burton, Seaside, Oregon

4 cups flour
2 teaspoons baking powder
¼ teaspoon salt
1½ cups granulated sugar
1 cup butter
1 teaspoon baking soda
½ cup buttermilk
3 eggs
1 teaspoon vanilla

Preheat oven to 400°F. In a large bowl, sift together flour, baking powder, and salt; set aside. In a medium bowl, cream sugar and butter until light. Add eggs one at a time; beating after each addition. Stir in vanilla. In a small bowl, dissolve baking soda in the buttermilk. Alternately combine dry ingredients and milk. Shape dough into a ball, cover with plastic wrap, and refrigerate 30 minutes. On a lightly floured board, roll dough to a ⅛-inch thickness. Cut out cookies with floured cookie cutters and place on a greased baking sheet. Bake 12 minutes or until golden brown. Cool on a wire rack. Makes 75 cookies.

MAPLE NUT COOKIES
Eva Gonya, Millinocket, Maine

3 cups flour
1 teaspoon baking powder
1 cup chopped walnuts
1½ cups chopped dates
1½ cups brown sugar
1 cup butter
3 eggs
1 teaspoon vanilla
1 teaspoon baking soda
½ cup hot water

Preheat oven to 350°F. In a large bowl, sift flour with baking powder. Stir in walnuts and dates. Set aside. In a medium bowl, cream brown sugar with butter. Add eggs one at a time, beating well after each addition. Stir in vanilla. Stir in baking soda dissolved in water. Gradually add flour mixture to butter mixture; stir until just combined. Drop dough by rounded teaspoons onto a greased cookie sheet. Bake 8 minutes or until edges begin to brown. Makes 72 cookies.

THE SUPREME WORTH OF T

O LIFE, LIBERTY AND THE PU

Silhouette

June Masters Bacher

A silhouette of Christmastime
Reflects upon the snow,
Crisscrossing shadows merrily
As shoppers come and go.
They skate across the silver sheen
Made by the fragile ice,
Dart in and out of evergreen
That fills the air with spice.
They meet and greet on every street;
Then silently they part,
Bulging with packages that show
Each shadow has a heart.

It's beginning to look a lot like Christmas. . . .

Rockefeller Center in New York City is decorated for the holidays.
Photograph by Henryk T. Kaiser/Grant Heilman.

FOR THE CHILDREN

December Song

Eileen Spinelli

Sing a song
    of snowy nights,
    of neighbors stringing
    twinkling lights,
    of sugar cookies
    shaped like stars,
    and trees tied
    to the roof of cars.

Sing a song
    of spangled kings
    and angels wearing
    wire wings,
    of paper boxes,
    silver bows,
    and gifts hid under
    attic clothes.

Sing of warm
    against the cold,
    of simple, peace-filled
    stories told,
    of drums that thump
    and bells that chime.
    Sing a song
    of Christmastime.

This Austrian holiday art depicts children happily busy with seasonal decorations. Image provided by Fine Art Photographic Library, Ltd., London.

READERS' REFLECTIONS

Christmas
Marion L. Williams
Cold Brook, New York

Each Christmas is a special time,
One that's set apart;
We think of loved ones and dear friends,
And joy fills every heart.
The crystal snowflakes in the air,
The decorations bright,
The soft, sweet songs of carolers
And church bells in the night—
Though days be short and bitter cold
And icy winds blow wild,
We feel once more the peace and love
Brought by that special Child.

Christmas Memories
Betty Vanhoozier
Madison Heights, Virginia

Oh, what a lovely Christmas tree
Standing there for all to see
And, beneath its fragrant boughs of green,
The prettiest presents ever seen.
Atop the tree shines the star bright,
Like that of the first Christmas night.
The tree is lovely, you will say,
As it stands there on Christmas Day;
Yet we need just a few things more,
Toys scattered upon the floor.
But the children are all grown;
They have families of their own.
Oh, if we could only hear
Their childish voices ringing clear,
"Look, Mom and Dad, come here and see
All that lies beneath our tree!"

Our Tree
Velma H. Chute

Behold our lovely Christmas tree;
It proudly stands for all to see.
Its lights of gold, red, blue, and green
Are glorious with their brilliant sheen.

Of colored ornaments, new and old,
Some wonderful stories can be told.
The children made them when they were young;
How happy they were when these were hung.

Observe the nativity scene;
It tells a lesson to you and me
Of Baby Jesus, a dear little stranger,
Born one night in a lonely manger.

All our children have grown and gone
And now have homes of their own;
But they recall when they were young,
The laughter, hopes, and carols sung

With family close, and prayers they said
As each was gently tucked into bed,
And dolls and toys beside them lay
Until they woke on Christmas Day.

Gifts
Carl E. Postel
Louisville, Kentucky

Christmas is the time of year
That I love best of all;
I love the bells and sounds I hear
And friends that come to call.

When Christmas comes with all its thrills,
A spirit fills the air;
Across the fields and snowy hills,
God's love is everywhere.

I love our family Christmas tree
And presents tied with bows;
My heart rejoices when I see
The way each candle glows.

I love the snow and lights on strings
And star-lit skies above.
But the very best of all these things
Are the smiles of those we love.

Readers are invited to submit original poetry for possible publication in future issues of
IDEALS. *Please send typed copies only; manuscripts will not be returned. Writers receive*
payment for each published submission. Send material to Readers' Reflections, Ideals
Publications, 535 Metroplex Drive, Suite 250, Nashville, Tennessee 37211.

CHRISTMAS ANGEL

Virginia Blanck Moore

Half of me wants to throw away
This angel with damaged wings,
Stored in the attic at Yuletide's end
With leftover Christmas things.

Half of me sees that the gold on her robe
Is tarnished beyond repair,
And obviously the sheen is gone
From her halo-crowned, golden hair.

But half of me treasures the memories
That crowd as I hold her near,
Memories of all the joys she has seen
From her treetop year after year.

So I climb the ladder and put her there
In what is her rightful place,
Forgetting the injuries the years
  have brought—
She still has her angel face.

Though the glow she once had
Through the years may depart,
She retains, as always,
Her hold on the heart.

This family room offers holiday hospitality.
Photograph by Jessie Walker.

FROM AMERICA'S ATTIC

D. Fran Morley and Maud Dawson

MEMORIES

My favorite old photograph is one of my grandmother, standing at her kitchen sink. Her hands are in the water, and she is laughing. That spontaneous picture preserves a moment from her everyday life. It captures her personality, and the sparkle in her eyes tells me that she probably had a good relationship with the photographer, my grandfather. This picture dates from about 1915.

Today, photography communicates news events, makes identifications, keeps travel and space records, and provides medical and scientific information, among other tasks. Even the arts, such as painting, architecture, and fashion, depend in some manner on photography. The average American, however, still thinks that a camera's importance is based on recording our individual lives and the events that are special to us. "Like to a coin, passing from hand to hand, / Are common memories. . . ." As the poet describes, we cherish our memories and thus share our photographs, passing them from one generation to another. Without the ubiquitous hand-held camera, the opportunity to revisit the past would certainly not be so easily available to us.

As the Greek words from which the word *photography* originated imply, "drawing with light" has fascinated people for hundreds of years. The sixteenth century's *camera obscura*, a darkened chamber with a tiny hole in one wall through which light entered and projected an upside-down image, is considered the earliest camera. By the nineteenth century, the camera had been reduced to a hand-held box with a lens and an angled mirror.

With that one-dollar camera in hand, anyone, even a child, could take pictures.

The early Daguerreotypes, invented in France, were made in an expensive process and only one picture came from each shot. If more than one picture was wanted, two cameras, side by side, were used at the same time, a rather cumbersome method of achieving duplicates. For many years, photographic equipment included, among other things, a heavy tripod, an enclosed space for spreading photograph emulsion on glass plates, chemicals, glass tanks, a heavy plate holder, and a jug of water.

In the late nineteenth century, however, at age twenty-four, George Eastman took on the task of simplifying photography and reducing the need for so much bulky equipment. While employed as a bank clerk, Eastman worked nights in his mother's kitchen for nearly three years, experimenting with chemicals and formulas. Finally, he developed a dry-plate formula for glass plates and patented a machine to make the plates. He opened his first business in Rochester, New York, in 1880. The new plates made developing photographs easier, but it was still work reserved for professionals and Eastman's ultimate goal was to make photography accessible to everyone.

The availability of roll film, in the late 1880s, made picture-taking even more simplified. In promoting use of this film, Eastman marketed a twenty-five dollar, small, black box camera with film already inside. Buyers could make the exposures and mail the camera, with the exposed film still inside, back to Eastman for developing. The camera would be returned, newly loaded with fresh film. The slogan, "You press the button, we do the rest," emphasized the ease of picture-taking and promoted the idea that a photograph could be taken without special training or awkward equipment. Today's disposable camera is the contemporary version of this concept.

Eastman named his new camera the Kodak because he thought the letter *k* was a "strong, incisive letter" and the name itself was short and memorable. In 1893, the Kodak Girl was introduced. She was a young, fashionable woman pictured in advertisements wearing a blue and white striped dress, always with a Kodak camera in hand, promoting the snapshot as a means of providing pleasing mementos of travel and special events.

In 1900, the release of the inexpensive Brownie camera, the first truly affordable and, more importantly, portable camera, marked a significant step toward Americans' adoption of informal photography. With that one-dollar camera in hand, anyone, even a child, could take pictures, and Americans chose to record their everyday lives.

The Brownie Camera, named after popular cartoon characters of the day, was one of the first mass-produced items in America, and it quickly

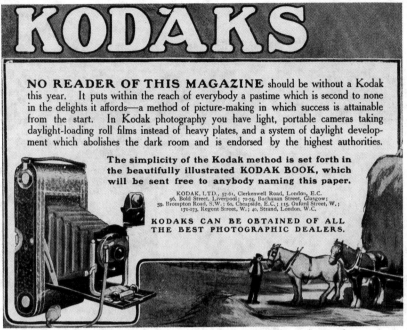

This early advertisement for Kodak highlights the importance of easy photography. Photograph from Retrofile/Robertstock.

became one of the most popular. Children were encouraged to join the Brownie Camera Club where they could enter contests and win prizes. More than 150,000 Brownie cameras were sold in the first year. In 1930, to celebrate the company's fiftieth anniversary, Eastman Kodak gave "A Gift to the Children of America," and offered a free Brownie camera and roll of film to any child who was twelve that year. A total of 500,000 cameras were distributed.

An entirely new method of taking photographs was introduced in 1947. An American physicist, Edwin Herbert Land, developed instant film and the first Polaroid Land Camera was on the market by 1948. His vision of instant pictures has been subsequently reflected in the popularity of digital cameras.

Hallmark cards first issued Christmas photo-holder cards in 1979, and today the tradition continues with many people sharing news and snapshots of family members during the holiday season. As I look at the photographs lined up along my desk, I see everyday moments, little slices of life, captured for all time, and to me these are priceless.

Around the Hearth

Mildred L. Jarrell

It's still the same old fireplace,
Yet it has a special glow;
A great Yule log is burning
That we dusted clean of snow.

And spread above the mantel,
Scents of holly sprigs and spruce
Are mingling with the woodsmoke
Beneath our dear old roof.

This winter night the firelight
Fills us with a sense of peace,
And we share the rich blessings
Of a love that does not cease.

Now on the eve of Christmas,
With carolers singing near,
The hearth fire gives to all within
Its gifts of warmth and cheer.

Christmas Eve

Gail Brook Burket

We light a log fire on the hearth
And gather round its cheer
To sing the carols long beloved
When Christmastime is here.
And at our window we have set
A gleaming candle light,
Whose golden beams will shine afar
To welcome Him tonight.

*A country dining room provides a
nice place to relax during the holidays.
Photograph by Jessie Walker.*

45

BITS & PIECES

Perhaps the best Yuletide decoration
is being wreathed in smiles.
—*Author Unknown*

Christmas! The very word
brings joy to our hearts.
—*Joan Winmill Brown*

Oh! Holly branch and mistletoe.
And Christmas chimes wherever we go.
And stockings pinned up in a row!
These are thy gifts, December!
—*Harriet R. Blodgett*

The best of all gifts around any Christmas tree: the
presence of a happy family all wrapped up in each other.
—*Burton Hillis*

Christmas may be a day of feasting, or of prayer, but
always it will be a day of remembrance—a day in
which we think of everything we have ever loved.
—*Augusta E. Rundel*

Christmas is the
season for kindling the
fire of hospitality in the
hall, the genial flame of
charity in the heart.

—*Washington Irving*

The holly and ivy about the walls wind
And show that we ought to our neighbors be kind.

—*Author Unknown*

The Christmas fires brightly gleam
And dance among the holly boughs.

—*Anne P. L. Field*

Then sing to the holly, the Christmas holly,
That hangs over peasant and king.

—*Eliza Cook*

So, now is come our joyfullest feast,
Let every man be jolly;
Each room with ivy leaves is drest,
And every post with holly.

—*George Wither*

47

The End of the Play

William Makepeace Thackeray

The play is done; the curtain drops,
    Slow falling to the prompter's bell:
A moment yet the actor stops,
    And looks around, to say farewell.
It is an irksome word and task;
    And, when he's laughed and said his say,
He shows, as he removes the mask,
    A face that's anything but gay.

One word, ere yet the evening ends,
    Let's close it with a parting rhyme,
And pledge a hand to all young friends,
    As fits the merry Christmastime.
On life's wide scene you, too, have parts
    That Fate ere long shall bid you play;
Good night! with honest gentle hearts
    A kindly greeting go always. . . .

Come wealth or want, come good or ill,
    Let young and old accept their part,
And bow before the Awful Will,
    And bear it with an honest heart,

Who misses or who wins the prize.
    Go, lose or conquer as you can;
But if you fail, or if you rise,
    Be each, pray God, a gentleman.

A gentleman, or old or young!
    (Bear kindly with my humble lays);
The sacred chorus first was sung
    Upon the first of Christmas Days:
The shepherds heard it overhead—
    The joyful angels raised it then:
Glory to Heaven on high, it said,
    And peace on earth to gentle men.

My song, save this, is little worth;
    I lay the weary pen aside
And wish you health, and love, and mirth,
    As fits the solemn Christmastide.
As fits the holy Christmas birth,
    Be this, good friends, our carol still—
Be peace on earth, be peace on earth,
    To men of gentle will.

Strike all your harps and set them ringing;
On hill and heath
Let every breath
Throw all its power into singing!
—PAUL LAURENCE DUNBAR

We Christmas caroled down the Vale,
    And up the Vale, and round the Vale;
    We played and sang that night
As we were yearly wont to do—
    A carol in a minor key,
        A carol in the major D,
Then at each house: "Good wishes:
    Many Christmas joys to you!"
—THOMAS HARDY

Golden bells make dainty ornaments for a Christmas tree.
Photograph by Michael W. Thomas/Grant Heilman.

A Merry Christmas from LITTLE WOMEN

Louisa May Alcott

Jo was the first to wake in the gray dawn of Christmas morning. No stockings hung at the fireplace, and for a moment she felt as much disappointed as she did long ago, when her little sock fell down because it was crammed so full of goodies. Then she remembered her mother's promise and, slipping her hand under her pillow, drew out a little crimson-covered book. She knew it very well, for it was that beautiful old story of the best life ever lived, and Jo felt that it was a true guidebook for any pilgrim going on a long journey.

She woke Meg with a "Merry Christmas" and bade her see what was under her pillow. A green-covered book appeared, with the same picture inside, and a few words written by their mother, which made their one present very precious in their eyes. Presently Beth and Amy woke to rummage and find their little books also, one dove-colored, the other blue, and all sat looking at and talking about them, while the east grew rosy with the coming day.

In spite of her small vanities, Margaret had a sweet and pious nature, which unconsciously influenced her sisters, especially Jo, who loved her very tenderly and obeyed her because her advice was so gently given.

"Girls," said Meg seriously, looking from the tumbled head beside her to the two little night-capped ones in the room beyond, "Mother wants us to read and love and mind these books, and we must begin at once. We used to be faithful about it, but since Father went away and all this war trouble unsettled us, we have neglected many things. You can do as you please, but I shall keep my book on the table here and read a little every morning as soon as I wake, for I know it will do me good and help me through the day."

Then she opened her new book and began to read. Jo put her arm round her and, leaning cheek to cheek, read also, with the quiet expression so seldom seen on her restless face.

"How good Meg is! Come, Amy, let's do as they do. I'll help you with the hard words, and they'll explain things if we don't understand," whispered Beth, very much impressed by the pretty books and her sisters' example.

"I'm glad mine is blue," said Amy. And then the rooms were very still while the pages were softly turned, and the winter sunshine crept in to touch the bright heads and serious faces with a Christmas greeting.

A warm fire adds cheer to this country living room. Photograph by Jessie Walker.

Christmas Eve Homage

Chris Ahlemann

The family walks with eager steps
Through gently falling snow
To where the small brick church awaits,
Its windows all aglow.

They enter then with earnest hearts
And quickly find a pew;
Their spirits stir at organ tones
Of carols old, yet new.

Each listens then in reverent awe
At the story which unfolds,
Of how Love came to earth one night
In a stable rude and cold.

Their heads then bow in silent prayer
While angels hover near,
And grateful hearts give up to God
The present of a tear.

And when at last it's time to go,
They leave with quiet joy;
For tonight their lives were born anew
As they glimpsed God's baby boy.

**I do not know a grander effect of
music on the moral feelings than
to hear the full choir and the
pealing organ performing a
Christmas anthem in a cathedral.
— Washington Irving**

*The Meeting House at Canaan, New Hampshire,
is beautifully framed by evergreens.
Photograph by William H. Johnson.*

Voices in the Mist

Alfred, Lord Tennyson

The time draws near the birth of Christ:
The moon is hid; the night is still;
The Christmas bells from hill to hill
Answer each other in the mist.

Four voices of four hamlets round,
From far and near, on mead and moor,
Swell out and fail, as if a door
Were shut between me and the sound:

Each voice four changes on the wind,
That now dilate, and now decrease,
Peace and goodwill, goodwill and peace,
Peace and goodwill, to all mankind.

Village Christmas

Loise Pinkerton Fritz

The village sits so still tonight;
In windows candles glow,
Emitting rays of warmest light
Upon new-fallen snow.
The air is still, so very still,
One cannot feel a wisp;
For on this very night of nights
The earth is silence-kissed.

So quietly small creatures tread
Upon the earth's white cloak,
And trusting hearts of friendly folk
Are filled with love and hope.
The village sits so still tonight,
So peaceful, solemn too.
A reverent aura here pervades:
Christmas is passing through.

Christmas lights at this home soften the winter evening.
Photograph by William H. Johnson.

55

THROUGH MY WINDOW

Pamela Kennedy

MARY'S JOURNEY

The dust danced in a golden sunbeam as the young girl studied the space just before her. She shook her head slightly. She wondered if she were dreaming. Then, with a rush, the experiences of a few moments ago swirled in her mind: the angel, the announcement, the question, the promise, her agreement. She raised her hand to her face. Somehow the familiar contours of her cheek and jaw reassured her. She was still Mary of Nazareth, betrothed to Joseph the carpenter. Then she caught her breath. She was also something else. She moved her hand to her waist and held it there a moment, hearing the echo of the heavenly messenger, "You shall conceive and bring forth a son, and shall call him Jesus. The Holy Spirit will come upon you and through the power of the Highest, the child you bear will be called the Son of God. Your cousin, Elisabeth, has also conceived a child in her old age. For with God, nothing is impossible."

Elisabeth! Mary gathered her shawl around her head and ran from the room. Gathering a few belongings, she quickly located a group of pilgrims who were traveling south towards Judea. Soon she could be at the hillside home of Zacharias and Elisabeth.

As she walked the dusty Galilean road, the angelic message tumbled in her mind. How could it be true? And yet, how could it not? Hundreds of years earlier had not the prophet Isaiah spoken of a holy child, a Messiah, born of a virgin? Surely, she was not that woman. But the angel told her she had found favor with God, that she was blessed. Impossible. Then she recalled his last few words: "With God, nothing is impossible." She hurried along, anxious to see her cousin.

Leaving the other travelers, Mary climbed

Mary's fears subsided in the warm glow of Elisabeth's love.

---

the path leading to the home of Zacharias. Bursting in the door she called "Elisabeth! Elisabeth! It's Mary!"

"Child!" the older woman cried. Mary's heart jumped as she saw the bulge of pregnancy under Elisabeth's robes. Then her cousin reached out to her. "Oh, Mary, you are truly blessed as is the child in your womb! How wonderful it is that the mother of my Lord should come to me! The moment I heard your greeting, the babe growing in me leaped for joy!"

Mary could not believe her ears. How could Elisabeth know? Mary was overwhelmed. It was true! Amazingly, impossibly, miraculously true! She laughed out loud and, recalling the words of Hannah from the ancient Scriptures, she burst forth: "My soul magnifies the Lord and my spirit rejoices in God, my Savior. For He that is mighty has done great things for me. Holy is His name."

She fell into the arms of Elisabeth, and the two of them stood there a long time, laughing and weeping for joy.

"Come," Elisabeth said finally, "you must stay with us. My child will not be born for a few more months. There is so much for us to talk about."

Mary's fears subsided in the warm glow of Elisabeth's love. Day after day they walked and talked about God and about the sons they would bear. They marveled at the mysteries of the Lord and how He could use them, two simple women, to accomplish His purposes. As Elisabeth's child grew, so did Mary's faith. How great was God's love!

All too quickly, three months passed. Mary knew she could not remain in Judea much longer. It was nearly time for Elisabeth's baby to be born and time for Mary to step into her own future. The day they parted was one of both sorrow and joy. The older woman gave the younger a bundle of carefully folded swaddling clothes, a gift for the unborn child. They embraced one last time, and then Mary turned and hurried down the hillside.

Turning her back on the safety of her relatives' home, she set her face towards Nazareth and the reality that lay before her. What would Joseph think? Would he believe her? What about their betrothal vows? Already she had felt the tiny flutter of new life within her womb. It was no longer just a possibility. She was most certainly with child. When she slept at night, huddled under the dark canopy of the summer sky, her dreams were filled with anxious visions.

Angels sang songs of praise to God, but their choruses were interrupted by the angry voices of townspeople calling out her shame. And Joseph, dear Joseph. His face appeared in her dreams as well. He was confused, disappointed, unbelieving.

In the morning she woke, braided her hair, and dusted off her cloak. Silently she prayed as she continued the last few miles into Nazareth. Then, as the town came into view, she felt the warm rays of the rising sun against her back. It felt like God's loving embrace, driving the fear and apprehension from her heart.

Mary raised her chin and set her eyes upon her home, her future. Then, as clearly as she had heard them the first time, the words of Gabriel echoed in her mind once more: "With God, nothing is impossible."

Pamela Kennedy is a freelance writer of short stories, articles, essays, and children's books. She has made her home with her husband and three children on both U.S. coasts and currently resides in Honolulu, Hawaii.

Original artwork by Doris Ettlinger.

THE ANNUNCIATION

Luke 1: 26–33

And in the sixth month the angel Gabriel was sent from God unto a city of Galilee, named Nazareth, to a virgin espoused to a man whose name was Joseph, of the house of David; and the virgin's name was Mary.

And the angel came in unto her, and said, Hail, thou that art highly favoured, the Lord is with thee: blessed art thou among women.

And when she saw him, she was troubled at his saying, and cast in her mind what manner of salutation this should be.

And the angel said unto her, Fear not, Mary: for thou hast found favour with God.

And, behold, thou shalt conceive in thy womb, and bring forth a son, and shalt call his name JESUS.

He shall be great, and shall be called the Son of the Highest: and the Lord God shall give unto him the throne of his father David:

And he shall reign over the house of Jacob for ever; and of his kingdom there shall be no end.

THE ANNUNCIATION *by John William Waterhouse (1849–1917). Image provided by Fine Art Photographic Library, Ltd., London.*

THE ATIVITY

Luke 2: 1–7

—m—

And it came to pass in those days, that there went out a decree from Caesar Augustus, that all the world should be taxed. (And this taxing was first made when Cyrenius was governor of Syria.)

And all went to be taxed, every one into his own city.

And Joseph also went up from Galilee, out of the city of Nazareth, into Judaea, unto the city of David, which is called Bethlehem; (because he was of the house and lineage of David:) to be taxed with Mary his espoused wife, being great with child.

And so it was, that, while they were there, the days were accomplished that she should be delivered.

And she brought forth her firstborn son, and wrapped him in swaddling clothes, and laid him in a manger; because there was no room for them in the inn.

NATIVITY by Charles Poerson (1609–1667). Photograph by Gérard Blot. Image provided by Art Resource NY/Réunion des Musées Nationaux/Louvre, Paris, France.

ANGELS AND SHEPHERDS

Luke 2: 8–14

And there were in the same country shepherds abiding in the field, keeping watch over their flock by night.

And, lo, the angel of the Lord came upon them, and the glory of the Lord shone round about them: and they were sore afraid.

And the angel said unto them, Fear not: for, behold, I bring you good tidings of great joy, which shall be to all people.

For unto you is born this day in the city of David a Saviour, which is Christ the Lord. And this shall be a sign unto you; Ye shall find the babe wrapped in swaddling clothes, lying in a manger.

And suddenly there was with the angel a multitude of the heavenly host praising God, and saying,

Glory to God in the highest, and on earth peace, good will toward men.

THE ADORATION OF THE SHEPHERDS *by Lorenzo Lotto (1480–1536). Photograph by Eric Lessing. Image provided by Art Resource NY/Musei Civici d'Arte e Storia/Brescia, Italy.*

ADORATION OF THE MAGI

Matthew 2: 7–12

—⁂—

Then Herod, when he had privily called the wise men, inquired of them diligently what time the star appeared.

And he sent them to Bethlehem, and said, Go and search diligently for the young child; and when ye have found him, bring me word again, that I may come and worship him also.

When they had heard the king, they departed; and, lo, the star, which they saw in the east, went before them, till it came and stood over where the young child was.

When they saw the star, they rejoiced with exceeding great joy.

And when they were come into the house, they saw the young child with Mary his mother, and fell down, and worshipped him: and when they had opened their treasures, they presented unto him gifts; gold, and frankincense, and myrrh.

And being warned of God in a dream that they should not return to Herod, they departed into their own country another way.

ADORATION OF THE MAGI by Antonio Balestra (1666–1740). Image provided by Cameraphoto/Art Resource/ S. Zaccaria, Venice, Italy.

THE FLIGHT INTO EGYPT

Matthew 2:13–15

And when they were departed, behold, the angel of the Lord appeareth to Joseph in a dream, saying, Arise, and take the young child and his mother, and flee into Egypt, and be thou there until I bring thee word: for Herod will seek the young child to destroy him.

When he arose, he took the young child and his mother by night, and departed into Egypt:

And was there until the death of Herod: that it might be fulfilled which was spoken of the Lord by the prophet, saying, Out of Egypt have I called my son.

FLIGHT INTO EGYPT *by Jacob Jordeans (1593–1678).*
Image provided by Christie's Images/SuperStock.

We consider **Christmas** as the encounter,
the great encounter, the historical
encounter, the decisive encounter, between
God and **mankind**. He who has faith
knows this truly; let him rejoice.

—Pope Paul VI, December 23, 1965

The Most Perfect Gift

Micheline Hull Dolan

No blanket of white
To cover the ground,
No pines brightly glowing
With lights all around,

No presents tied gaily
With ribbon of red,
Just a pillow of straw
For the infant's sweet head.

A mother's sweet song
Broke the silence that night.
A brilliant white star
Turned darkness to light.

The birth in the manger,
Pure love we recall,
God's most perfect Christmas
Gift to us all.

*The vibrant red and green of holly accent the garden
at Oak Hill Plantation in Mount Berry, Georgia.
Photograph by William H. Johnson.*

69

A Christmas Carol

Josiah Gilbert Holland

There's a song in the air!
    There's a star in the sky!
    There's a mother's deep prayer
    And a baby's low cry!
And the star rains its fire while the Beautiful sing,
For the manger of Bethlehem cradles a king.

    There's a tumult of joy
    O'er the wonderful birth,
    For the virgin's sweet boy
    Is the Lord of the earth.
Ay! the star rains its fire and the Beautiful sing,
For the manger of Bethlehem cradles a king.

    In the light of that star
    Lie the ages impearled;
    And that song from afar
    Has swept over the world.
Every hearth is aflame, and the Beautiful sing
In the homes of the nations that Jesus is King.

    We rejoice in the light,
    And we echo the song
    That comes down through the night
    From the heavenly throng.
Ay! we shout to the lovely evangel they bring,
And we greet in his cradle our Savior and King.

Red poinsettias, the traditional Christmas decoration, are even more striking in clusters. Photograph by William H. Johnson.

DEVOTIONS FROM THE HEART

Pamela Kennedy

But after he had considered this, an angel of the Lord appeared to him in a dream and said, "Joseph son of David, do not be afraid to take Mary home as your wife, because what is conceived in her is from the Holy Spirit." Matthew 1:19–20 (NIV)

GOD HAS A BETTER IDEA

I have often thought that Joseph is a somewhat overlooked participant of the Christmas story. There he was, minding his own business in the carpenter shop, contemplating his engagement, when suddenly his fiancée, Mary, takes off for a three-month visit to her cousin, Elisabeth; and when Mary returns, she announces she is expecting. This would be shocking enough news to report in our day and age; but back in the first century, it could have been been grounds for a death sentence!

Joseph faces a very serious dilemma. According to the customs and practices of his time, he has two options: He could divorce Mary quietly for breaking their engagement vows, which are as binding as marriage vows, or he could denounce her publicly and hand her over to the religious leaders, who have the legal authority to call for her death by stoning. His decision places him both at the sidelines and at the center of a huge drama. He had to have wondered, who is the father of Mary's baby? What has Mary done? What should he do?

We know from Matthew's account that Joseph was a man who considered things care-

fully. He was not impulsive, nor was he arrogant. After weighing his options, Joseph decides he will divorce Mary quietly. Although people might assume that he was weak, or worse, complicit in this apparent moral indiscretion, Joseph is unwilling to see Mary punished or publicly disgraced. Joseph's primary concern is not for himself; it is for the woman

---

*Dear Father, this Advent season
let me set aside my own ideas
long enough to ask what You would
have me do. Then give me the courage
and humility I need to follow
the path You set before me. Amen.*

---

he loves. Joseph's decision exposes his character and leaves room for God's compassion.

In the dark night of Joseph's contemplation, God sends an angel who presents Joseph with a third option. For Joseph to accept this angelic revelation requires both faith and courage. He must believe the word of God and step away from the dictates of his culture. And Joseph

Photograph by Dennis Frates.

again proves himself a man of integrity. He agrees that God has a better plan for him; and, in faith, he steps out to take Mary's hand in marriage. Together, they walk into their future.

How often do we ourselves struggle with decisions that seem difficult and overwhelming? We cast about in our minds for solutions, weighing one option against another, trying to determine the best course of action. What should we do when faced with difficult dilemmas? Should we assert what we believe to be our rights or choose to submit to the will of another? Should we demand justice or extend mercy? What if we considered the way of Joseph and opened our hearts to the possibility that God might have another, better idea? What if we set aside our own

agendas and prayerfully waited, in the dark night of our uncertainty, for the Lord to reveal his plan? Could it be that in our searching we would discover, just as Joseph does, that God has a better plan for us?

This Christmas, revel in the triumphant song of the angels and the expectant awe of the shepherds. Wonder at the impossible miracle worked by God in the life of a young Galilean girl. Journey with the Magi along the path of wisdom in search of a King and Savior. And remember to appreciate the gentle courage of Joseph, who set aside his own decisions in order to embrace the plans of God. Be brave enough to admit, in the midst of your personal quandaries, that God just might have a better idea.

A Hymn Sung as by the Shepherds

Richard Crashaw

We saw Thee in Thy balmy nest,
    Bright dawn of our eternal day!
We saw Thine eyes break from their East
    And chase the trembling shades away.
We saw Thee and we blessed the sight;
We saw Thee by Thine own sweet light.

Welcome, all wonders in one sight!
    Eternity shut in a span,
Summer in winter, day in night,
    Heaven in earth and God in man;
Great little one! whose all embracing birth
Lifts earth to heaven, stoops heaven to earth.

To Thee, meek Majesty, soft King,
    Of simple graces and sweet loves,
Each of us his lamb will bring,
    Each his pair of silver doves,
Till burnt at last in fire of Thy fair eyes
Ourselves become our own best sacrifice.

Sunset makes this dairy farm a wonderland of color. Photograph by Larry LeFever/Grant Heilman.

Weathervanes FOR Steeples

Ralph W. Seager

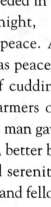

In Guyanoga valley we located a farmer by his big, red barn; it was his landmark, his identity and signature. His house showed up later. Folks would answer queries by saying, "Yep, that's White's barn up there on East Hill," or, "Cole's is the first barn up Belknap Hill." A stranger might wonder whether he would find a house at all, and he would have to wonder until he got there. The first thing to know about a Guyanoga farmer was where his barn sat. Everything else came in second.

His silo was nearly as significant, standing like a lighthouse far from sea, yet raised in that white imagery. When the sun got tired and dropped its head on the shoulders of evening, these silos would catch the last rays upon their domes, light up, and become beacons across the western side of day. It was then that the farmers would turn their plows at dusk and head for home.

Many a Guyanoga boy first learned the meaning of *holy* and *sacred* not in church, but within his father's barn. He came face-on with Christmas the night the baby lamb was born. When Old Dobbin was down in his stall and could not get up, he came to grips with his own Gethsemane. Before he could spell the word or know its meaning, he was down on his blue-patched knees asking for it not to happen. Easter came first—handed to him when his new calf stood up on knobby stilts all wet and shining and trembling, and the boy trembled too, seeing that life was getting better than ever.

This was his first church. Here he became acquainted with birth and life and death, with the peace of animals upon it all. He learned about barns and granaries and bushels, sheep and horses, the cattle on a thousand hills, doves on the rafters, the mice under the threshing floor; for none of these creatures had given up on the Bible. They were still in it as they have been for thousands of years. They always will be.

The first and best barn we know cradled the Light of the World. Yet, across the print of literature, the hounds of prejudice and bigotry have always snapped at the innkeeper. Here was a man who knew that whatever else Mary needed in that wide night, she needed peace. And there was peace in the stable: the peace of cudding cows, of gentle ewes. Farmers of every age know that this man gave the best he had, his barn, better by far than the inn. For the stable offered serenity against turmoil, sharing against greed, and fellowship against selfishness.

At the inn was confusion amid the stifling press of humanity. There was contention for

THE FIRST AND BEST BARN WE KNOW CRADLED THE LIGHT OF THE WORLD.

A barn shall harbour heaven,
A stall become a shrine.
—*Richard Wilbur*

In the William L. Finley National Wildlife Refuge in Oregon, this barn stands out against the expanse of snow. Photograph by Dennis Frates.

rooms and most assuredly the flaring of tempers of ill-tempered men. For no one, at any time, is happy on his way to pay taxes. So the innkeeper has lived under the condemnation of most of his fellowmen because he alone had the sense to lead Mary and Joseph to the peace of his mangers, into the warm fragrance of summer, the soft lowing of his cattle, and the white softness of sheep. Where would one find a better beginning for the Good Shepherd? Make no mistake about it, the world owes a debt to the keeper of the inn.

From that time to this, farmers have walked backwards through Christmas. They have reversed the original and have brought the bleating life of their barns into their kitchens. Down through the ages it has fallen to the farmer, he of the countryside, to act out Christmas over and over again. Every time he wraps the new-born lamb in his sweater, bedding it down in the woodbox behind the stove, he has renewed Christmas.

The Christmas Star

Charles A. Heath

Upon a still and starry night
Whose very stillness thrilled
The watch of centuries—the night
When hope would be fulfilled—
Through silent skies
A starlight flies
That God Eternal willed.

While eager eyes first caught its ray
To ages long denied—
Unlike the night, unlike the day,
But glory glorified—
Through singing skies
Hope verifies
That earth is now its sway.

Around heaven high the chorus rang,
Until earth, too, was filled,
For men joined angels as they sang—
So much their hearts were thrilled—
'Neath star-bright skies
The harmonies
No centuries have stilled.

The Holy Star

William Cullen Bryant

As shadows cast by cloud and sun
Flit o'er the summer grass,
So, in Thy sight, Almighty One,
Earth's generations pass.

And while the years, an endless host,
Come pressing swiftly on,
The brightest names that earth can boast
Just glisten and are gone.

Yet doth the Star of Bethlehem shed
A luster pure and sweet,
And still it leads, as once it led,
To the Messiah's feet.

O Father, may that holy star
Grow every year more bright,
And send its glorious beams afar
To fill the world with light.

*Christmas ornaments are a small but lovely part of the
holiday celebrations. Photograph by Nancy Matthews.*

I, SHORTER-LIVED THAN ANY TREE,
CAN STAND AND FEEL ETERNITY
WHEEL ABOUT ME IN THE FAR,
LONELY ORBIT OF A STAR.
—ROBERT P. TRISTRAM COFFIN

Winter Starlight

Hal Borland

Winter starlight has the deep fire glow of eternity, the unending gleam of wonder. To walk abroad on such nights is to walk in the midst of infinity. There are no limits to either time or distance, except as man himself may make them. I have but to touch the wind to know these things; for the wind itself is full of starlight, even as the frosted earth underfoot, starlight and endless time and exalted wonder.

My eye is caught by the red-gold star we call Arcturus, and wonder grows. Even as the ancients, I strain for a closer look through this peephole, this spark-burn in the blanket of night, hoping for the slightest glimpse into the dazzling brilliance of Beyond. I turn to the star called Betelgeuse, even redder than Arcturus, and I accept the factual truths of the astronomers and yet wonder if they constitute the whole, the ultimate truth. Time, and distance, and wonder—I walk up this valley in the midst of eternity.

Star after star—the night is filled with starlight, and the Milky Way is a whole sky-drift of mingled stardust. It is as though the star-studded wind were forever blowing across the deepest darkness, forever and changing only with the repeated seasons. Tonight it is thus, and tomorrow it will be a little changed, but only in relationship to me and my sense of time, and the next day another small notch of change. Yet another December will be the same again, as it has been before and still before.

I wonder and watch the winter stars, and there is starlight in my very puffs of life-breath. My shoulders lift toward the stars, for I, too, am a part of this eternity.

Moonset at dawn in Cleveland National Forest, California, is a breathtaking moment. Photograph by Christopher Talbot Frank.

Beneath the Winter Stars

Grace Noll Crowell

How white the stars are in this inky blackness!
How strangely still the hills and hollows lie!
How cold beneath the passionless white fires
That burn like molten silver in the sky!
I am so small beneath their countless numbers,
So little and so lost in this vast dark;
I reach my hands to find some warmth and comfort
In fires a million light years off, each spark
Left smoldering from the white heat of creation:
Strange, icy flames that have the power to sear
Upon my heart how truly unimportant
Is this small earth and man's brief sojourn here. . . .
And yet, and yet, recalling God's great mercy
In sending Christ to tread this planet's sod,
I straighten in the starlight; I grow taller,
Remembering my significance to God.

When I Heard the Learn'd Astronomer

Walt Whitman

When I heard the learn'd astronomer,
When the proofs, the figures, were ranged in columns before me,
When I was shown the charts and diagrams, to add, divide, and measure them,
When I, sitting, heard the astronomer where he lectured with much applause
      in the lecture-room,
How soon unaccountable I became tired and sick,
Till rising and gliding out I wander'd off by myself,
In the mystical moist night-air, and from time to time,
Looked up in perfect silence at the stars.

Sunrise on Redfish Lake, Sawtooth National Recreation Area, Idaho, is a natural masterpiece. Photograph by Carr Clifton.

THE NEW YEAR

Gladys Taber

What the new year will bring, we cannot know. I think of the year that has been folded away in time. There has been much good in it, although some sorrow; but there are always, in any year, many lovely memories, and I shall cherish them. Life is not, for most of us, a pageant of splendor but is made up of many small things, rather like an old-fashioned piecework quilt. No two people have the same, but we all have our own, whether it be listening to Beethoven's Fifth with a beloved friend or seeing a neighbor at the back door with a basket of white dahlias. Or after a long, hard day having the family say, "That was a good supper."

As the clock moves irrevocably from yesterday to today, I go out on the terrace and fill my heart with the intensity of the winter moonlight. This is the time when the heart is at peace and the spirit rests. I think of the words, "Be still, and know that I am God." Far off a branch falls in the old orchard, and sometimes a plane goes overhead bound for a far destination. I wish the pilot well, in that cold sky, and hope the passengers come safely home. Silently I say, "Happy New Year to all of us, all over this turning earth. And may we make it a year of loving-kindness and gentle hearts."

Snow blankets a country road, yet travelers still find their way.
Photograph by Larry LeFever/Grant Heilman.

85

READERS' FORUM

Snapshots from our IDEALS readers

Right: Alexandria Elizabeth Evans, daughter of Craig and Catherine Evans of Columbia, Illinois, offers her own mittens to the friendly snowman. Her great-grandmother, Dorothy Hoffman, shares this photograph with *Ideals*.

Below: Cousin Elves! Thelma Oldenburger of Wheaton, Illinois, sent *Ideals* this photograph of her two great-granddaughters, Mary and Michaela, dressed to play Santa's helpers.

Top right: "Need some help, Santa?" Jackson Brutzman, son of Christian and Erin Brutzman, of Tega Cay, South Carolina, is ready for Christmas. Great-grandmother Anna-Laura Laird shares this snapshot with *Ideals* readers.

Right: Two-year-old Claire Olivia Hefner of Sherrills Ford, North Carolina, is a Christmas fairy in finery, according to her grandmother, Rita Cannup, of Newport News, Virginia.

Below: The biggest bubble of all is the one that enchants fifteen-month-old Jacob Books. He is the son of Elmer and Karen Books of Phoenixville, Pennsylvania. Joan M. Books of Cleona, Pennsylvania, is the proud grandmother.

THANK YOU for sharing your family snapshots with *Ideals*. We hope to hear from other readers who would like to share theirs with the *Ideals* family. Please include a self-addressed, stamped envelope if you would like the photos returned; or, keep your originals for safekeeping and send duplicates, along with your name, address, and telephone number to:

Readers' Forum
Ideals Publications
535 Metroplex Drive, Suite 250
Nashville, Tennessee 37211

Dear Reader,

Our family actually has many Christmas trees. One we decorate at home, of course. The second is a public one, an angel tree from which each of us takes an envelope with a wish from a child. A third tree we share belongs to my in-laws, who ask my son and daughter to help decorate it and then serve them a meal of their favorite dishes in thanks for their help. Now college students, both my children continue to help their father with the Christmas celebration at a local children's home that always has a large tree decorated by the young people. Neighbors and friends have invited us to share dinners around their trees too.

At our home, the Christmas tree has traditionally remained standing through the first day of the New Year. The decorations are mostly remnants of our family history, beginning with the paper ornaments crafted by the children many years ago. The children spend more time now away, so they like to reminisce when we spend an evening placing our familiar ornaments on the tree.

The task of removal is mine alone. But reliving family memories makes this task ultimately enjoyable. Ulysses, our allergy-beleaguered cat, once tested his ability to scale the top of the tree and scattered ornaments and strings of light everywhere as he sneezed. Curly Joe, our black cocker spaniel, shoved packages and hid under the low, long branches of the Christmas tree, often accompanied by my son.

This year's family tree has become dry and brittle from its long vigil in the family room. Soon it will be towed outside and propped against the stone wall as a refuge for birds and then eventually donated to local parks to be ground into trail mulch. There is comfort in remembering the purposes of the trees in our Christmas holidays.

Marjorie L. Lloyd

ideals

Publisher, Patricia A. Pingry
Editor, Marjorie Lloyd
Designer, Marisa Calvin
Copy Editor, Marie Brown
Permissions Editor, Patsy Jay
Contributing Writers, Maud Dawson, Joan Donaldson, Richard Keller, Pamela Kennedy, D. Fran Morley, Patricia A. Pingry

ACKNOWLEDGMENTS

BACHER, JUNE MASTERS. "Silhouette." Used by permission of George W. Bacher. BORLAND, HAL. "Winter Starlight" from *This Hill, This Valley.* Copyright © 1957 by Hal Borland. Used by permission of Frances Collin, Literary Agent. BURKET, GAIL BROOK. "Christmas Eve." Used by permission of Anne E. Burket. CROWELL, GRACE NOLL. "Beneath the Winter Stars" from *Facing the Stars.* Copyright © 1941 by Harper & Brothers; renewed © 1968 by Grace Noll Crowell. Used by permission of HarperCollins Publishers. GUEST, EDGAR A. "Sleigh Bells" from *All In a Lifetime* by Edgar A. Guest. Published by Reilly & Lee Co., 1938. Used by permission of M. Henry Sobell, III. JARRELL, MILDRED L. "Winter Patterns" and "Around the Hearth." Used by permission of Serena Naumann. ODUM, MAMIE OZBURN. "Hitch Old Dobbin To the Sleigh." Used by permission of Mariann Holland. TABER, GLADYS. "The New Year" from *Stillmeadow Calendar.* Copyright © 1967 by Gladys Taber. Published by J. B. Lippincott. Used by permission of Brandt & Hochman Literary Agents, Inc. We sincerely thank those authors, or their heirs, some of whom we were unable to locate, who submitted original poems or articles to *Ideals* for publication. Every possible effort has been made to acknowledge ownership of material used.

Inside back cover: *In this painting by George Hinke, poinsettias frame the star over Bethlehem.*